HAYDN

THE FIRST BOOK FOR PIANISTS

Edited by

George Lucktenberg

CONTENTS

"Hob." refers to the scholar A. van Hoboken, whose numbering system for Haydn's works is used in place of "Opus" numbers in modern editions.

The selections included in this book are taken from "HAYDN – An Introduction to his Keyboard Works." For students and teachers who prefer an expanded introductory section and additional selections in a 64 page book, the publisher recommends the Haydn introduction listed above.

Born in the same year as George Washington, Joseph Haydn's life spanned the transition from Baroque to Classic style; and, more than any other single personality, he was responsible for shaping the new Classic style. The late 18th century was the time when the large instrumental forms—sonata, quartet, symphony—were the main challange to the composer. Haydn's slow-maturing genius assimilated all the trends, and consolidated them in an individual style that was both inspired and disciplined.

He is the earliest composer whose music has been played continuously from his own time down to ours, without a blank period and then a "rediscovery." He was without question the most famous composer in Europe between 1780 and 1810, and was also known in the original 13 United States.

Since his death, he has been known mainly for a small handful of favorite symphonies, string quartets, and piano sonatas. Actually, his piano sonatas include many little-known gems, some from as early as the 1760s, which are ideal for amateurs and students, and worth more attention from professionals as well. Although not a virtuoso player, he knew and liked the piano, which was developed during his lifetime. His solos and trios offer the pianist interesting features and endless musical delights.

All of the pieces in this book are in their original form, unsimplified. They have been thoroughly researched from their original manuscripts and/or the earliest editions. All of the notes, etc, in dark print are from the original sources. The indications in light gray print are editorial suggestions based on careful study of the performance practices of Haydn's day.

D1279836

ALLEGRO MODERATO IN C MAJOR

Hob. XVI:7

ANDANTE IN G MAJOR

Hob. XVI:8

SCHERZO IN F MAJOR

Hob. XVI:9

FINALE, FROM SONATA IN A MAJOR

Hob. XVI:12

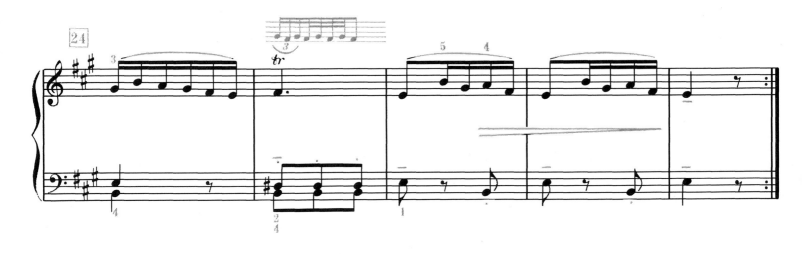

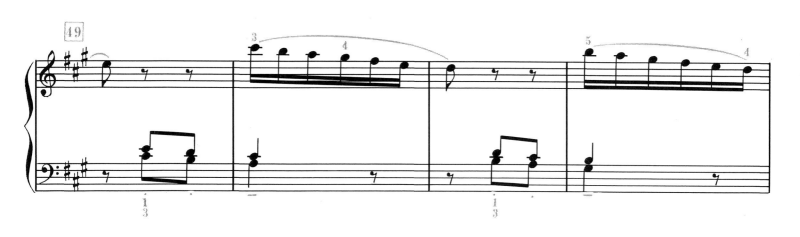

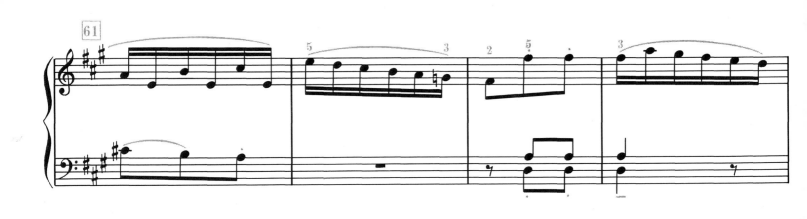

MINUET AND TRIO IN C

Hob. XVI:3

Trio

Menuet Da Capo

MENUET & TRIO AND FINALE,
FROM SONATA IN A MAJOR

(a) **Menuet al Rovescio** ♩ 144

Hob. XVI:26

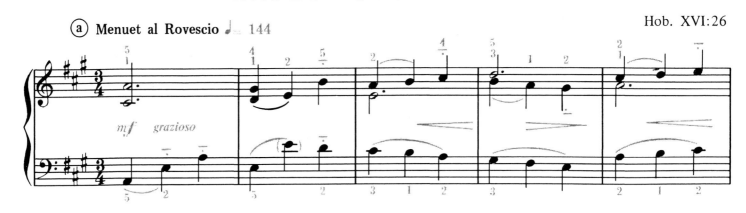

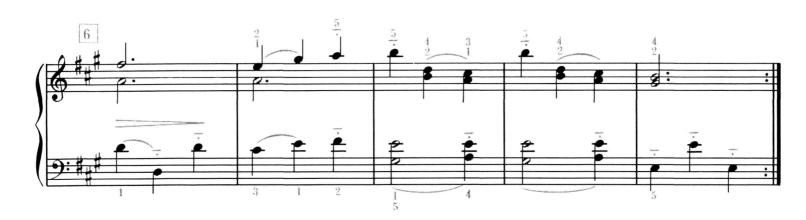

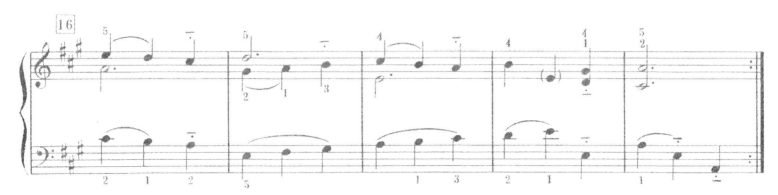

(a) The designation *"al Rovescio"* means that in both Menuet and Trio, the second half (m. 11-20; 33-44) is the exact reverse of the first strain—in the original, the second strain did not even appear in print, the player having to read it backwards!

Menuet Da Capo

MINUET AND TRIO,
FROM SONATA IN G MAJOR

Hob. XVI:6

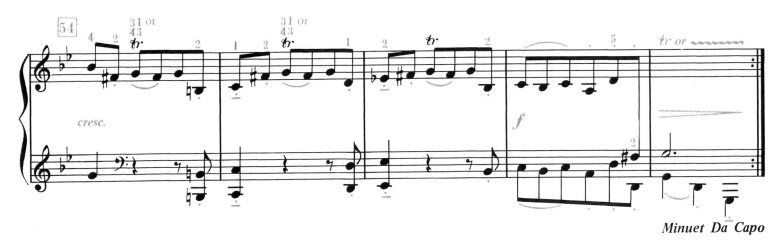

Minuet Da Capo

ARIETTA AND VARIATIONS IN A MAJOR

Hob. XVII:2

Var. II

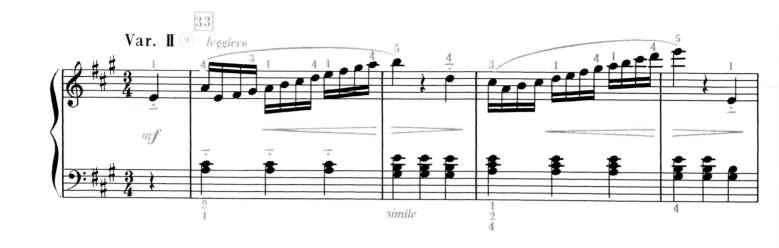

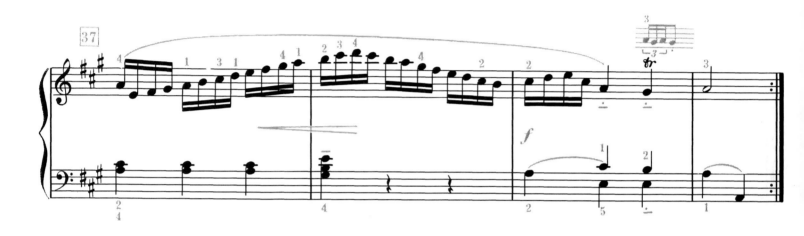

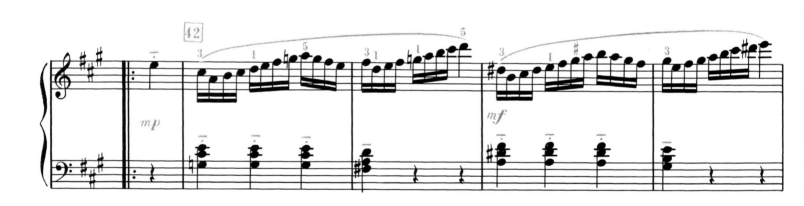

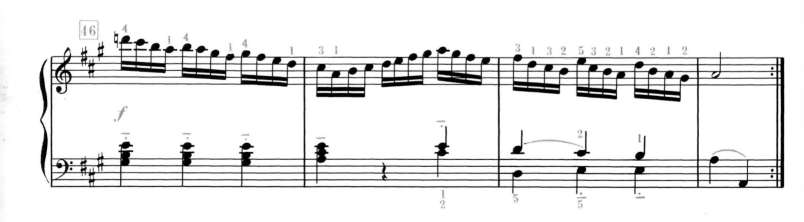

ⓐ May be omitted by less advanced students.

Var. Ⅲ Poco meno mosso

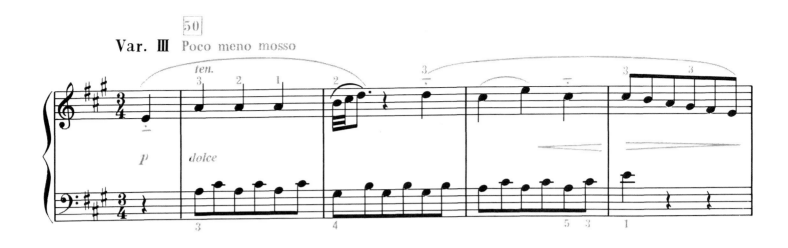

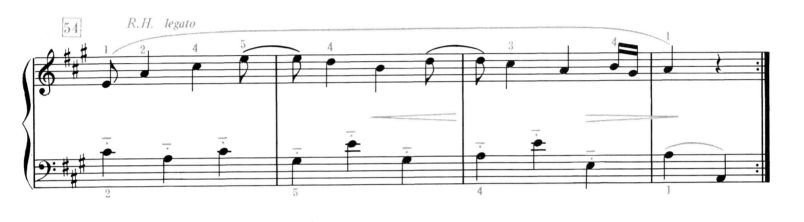

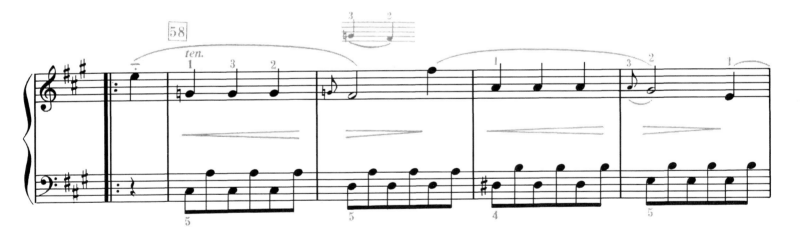

@ This variation is included only in the later of the two primary sources. See footnote on the next page (Var. VI).

(a) This variation is included in the Artaria printing of 1789; however, it was not among those in the more extensive "Oeuvres Complettes" printing twenty years later, and its authenticity may therefore be questioned. This editor believes it to be genuine.